The Greatest Christmas Ever

A Treasury of Inspirational Ideas and Insights for an Unforgettable Christmas

Honor Books
P. O. Box 55388
Tulsa, OK 74155

Unless otherwise indicated, all Scripture quotations are taken from the *King James Version* of the Bible.

The Scripture quotation marked NIV is taken from *The Holy Bible: New International Version*. Copyright © 1973, 1978, 1984 by The International Bible Society. Used by permission of Zondervan Bible Publishers.

The Greatest Christmas Ever:
A Treasury of Inspirational Ideas and
Insights for an Unforgettable Christmas
ISBN 1-56292-114-2
Copyright © 1995 by Honor Books, Inc.
P.O. Box 55388
Tulsa, Oklahoma 74155

Introduction

Finally! A great stocking stuffer that's sure to become a memorable family tradition in itself. *The Greatest Christmas Ever* sparkles with the charm of a lighted, tinseled Christmas tree. It crackles with the good feeling of an old-fashioned wood-burning fire. It rings forth with the familiar voice of home, calling together loved ones for a cherished moment of warmth and closeness.

What do *you* enjoy at Christmas time? Carols? Poems? Humor? Inspiration? Tasty recipes? Fun and creative gift ideas? It's all here! This memorable treasury of holiday inspiration and fun promises you, the reader, lovely thoughts, happy moments, creative ideas, and tasty recipes.

Tuck this little book of joy in among the gifts you give this holiday season. Share it with friends and loved ones as a holiday remembrance of years gone by. Share its Christmas spirit with all those wearied by the bustle of the busy holiday season. Watch the smiles burst onto the faces of young and old alike!

Oh, yes. . . don't forget to take this classic keepsake volume home to add to your own personal Christmas keepsakes, so you, too, can partake of *The Greatest Christmas Ever* for years and years to come.

No warm, downy pillow His sweet head pressed;
No soft garments His fair form dressed;
He lay in a manger, this Heavenly Stranger,
The precious Lord Jesus, the wonderful Child.

—Unknown

The Most Important Things You Can Give on Christmas

1. Your time — Volunteer to help those less fortunate.

2. Your love — It's the thought that counts.

3. Your life — Jesus was born that you might be saved.

4. Your Lord — Share Jesus with your friends and family.

The Greatest Christmas Ever

When Christmas lights shine forth upon
The glistening, new-blown snow,
While gifts hang low upon the tree
And shed love's golden glow,
When Christmas carols sound afar
Throughout the holy night,
God grant you sweet assurance that
His ways are always right!

—Leroy Victor Cleveland

Used by permission of Sword of the Lord Publishers
An Imprint of Sword of the Lord Publishing

GOOD QUESTION

A youngster received a red wagon for Christmas, and for days he went nowhere without it. But one afternoon he was happily rolling it along the front sidewalk when his father called, "Take that wagon in back and play with it. Remember, it's Sunday."

The boy started to obey, then turned around and with a puzzled look asked, "Isn't it Sunday in the back yard, too?"

—Agnes Kaminsky

Christmas Tree Decorating Theme Old - Fashioned:

1. Multi-colored lights.

2. Family ornaments hand-made and collected throughout the years.

3. Sprinkles of silver tinsel.

4. Highlights of red and white candy canes.

5. A light puff of snow over the branches.

6. An angel on top.

*H*e brought peace on earth and wants
to bring it also into your soul—that peace
which the world cannot give. He is the One
who would save His people from their sins.

—Corrie ten Boom

Christmas Joys: A Treasury of Old Favorites and New Gems of Christmas Lo:
Legend, and Inspiration by Joan Winmill Brown
New York: Doubleday & Company, 1982

NO GLASS BETWEEN

The story is told of a little boy whose family was very poor. He received no gifts at Christmastime, but he spent what time he could looking in the store windows at the pretty things other little boys could have, but he couldn't.

One day he was run over by a car and taken to a hospital. One of the nurses bought him a toy, a troop of soldiers. As he touched them, what do you think he said? "There isn't any glass between!"

Some day we shall see Christ face to face, with no "glass" in between.

—Unknown

Used by permission of Sword of the Lord Publishers
An Imprint of Sword of the Lord Publishers

Things in General Never To Give for Christmas:

1. Fruitcakes — Remember the golden rule.

2. Neckties — Silk is okay.

3. Clothes — Size and personal taste vary too much.

4. Towels and washcloths — They rarely match the decor.

5. Loud or messy toys — Tambourines and paint, for instance.

Reflect upon your present blessings, of which every man has plenty; not on your past misfortunes, of which all men have some.

—Charles Dickens

Christmas Joys: A Treasury of Old Favorites and New Gems of Christmas Lo:
Legend, and Inspiration by Joan Winmill Brown
New York: Doubleday & Company, 1982.

Things To Do When Company Drops in:

1. Invite them in with a Christmas smile!

2. For atmosphere, put on a favorite instrumental Christmas tape.

3. Then light a fire in the woodburning fireplace, if you have one.

4. Offer a variety of treats on a festive holiday platter.

5. Sit by the fire for friendly conversation, and *relax*!

13

CHRISTMAS CHOCOLATE CHEWIES

1 package devil's food cake mix, 18.25 oz.
1 small package semi-sweet chocolate chips
1/2 cup vegetable shortening
2 large eggs, lightly beaten
1 tablespoon water
1/2 cup sifted powdered sugar
Candy sprinkles

*C*ombine first 5 ingredients in a large bowl, stirring until smooth. Shape dough into 1-inch balls, and roll in powdered sugar. Place 2 inches apart on lightly greased cookie sheets. Bake at 375° for 10 minutes. Remove from oven. Sprinkle with candy sprinkles. Cool 10 minutes on cookie sheets; remove to wire racks to cool completely.

Used by permission of Oxmoor House/Southern Progress
An Imprint of Oxmoor House Publishing

The Greatest Christmas Ever

"FORGIVE US OUR CHRISTMASES "

*T*he story has been published of a little girl caught in the pre-Christmas swirl of activity, all of which seemed to be coming to a head on Christmas Eve. Dad, loaded down with bundles, seemed to have an even greater number of worries. Mom, under the pressure of getting ready for the great occasion, had yielded to tears several times during the day. The little girl herself, trying to help, found that she was always under foot, and sometimes adult kindness to her wore thin.

Finally, near tears herself, she was hustled off to bed. There kneeling to pray the Lord's Prayer before finally tumbling in, her mind and tongue betrayed her and she prayed, "Forgive us our Christmases as we forgive those who Christmas against us."

Perhaps the little girl's prayer was not such a great mistake. Too often we leave out the Christ of Christmas. Too often He is crowded out of our busy lives. Remember, the best gift won't be found in a box but in a person.

—Unknown

Used by permission of Sword of the Lord Publishers
An Imprint of Sword of the Lord Publishers

MOCK CHAMPAGNE HOLIDAY PUNCH

- 2 bottles nonalcoholic sparkling white grape juice, chilled, 25.4 oz. ea.
- 2 bottles ginger ale, chilled, 2-liters ea.
- 1 bottle white grape juice, chilled, 32 oz.
- 1 can frozen lemonade concentrate, thawed and undiluted, 6 oz.
- 1 small jar maraschino cherries

Ice ring (optional)

*C*ombine all ingredients in a large punch bowl; add an ice ring, if desired.

Used by permissio of Oxmoor House/Southern Progress
An Imprint of Oxmoor House Publishing

Making Christmas Bright for Family Members Far Away:

1. In November, create a "Care Package." Send it by the first weekend in December.
2. Include a dated ornament for each person, uniquely fitted to each individual's interests.
3. Include a holiday newsletter personalized with hand-written notes from each of your family members to theirs.
4. Holiday wrap a cassette tape or video of your family singing or sharing current family events.
5. Include candies or cookies which your family made together with their family in mind.

THE PROPHECY

*F*or unto us a child is born, unto us a son is given: and the government shall be upon his shoulder: and his name shall be called Wonderful, Counsellor, The mighty God, The everlasting Father, The Prince of Peace. Of the increase of his government and peace there shall be no end, upon the throne of David, and upon his kingdom, to order it, and to establish it with judgment and with justice from henceforth even for ever. . . .

—Isaiah 9:6,7

Keeping Jesus the Focus of the Season:

1. Once a day during December, thank God for His Son and His gift of eternal life.
2. Incorporate the simplicity and peace of the true Christmas spirit into your holiday.
3. Begin one new tradition this year which incorporates the true meaning of Christmas.
4. Make a birthday cake out of breakfast breads. Serve it Christmas morning while everyone sings Happy Birthday to Jesus.
5. Take turns with your family members reading the Christmas story from the second chapter of Luke before opening gifts.

The very purpose of Christ's coming into the world was that He might offer up His life as a sacrifice for the sins of men. He came to die. This is the heart of Christmas.

—Rev. Billy Graham

Christmas Joys: A Treasury of Old Favorites and New Gems of Christmas Lo:
Legend, and Inspiration by Joan Winmill Brown
New York: Doubleday & Company, 1982.

Making Christmas Fun and Memorable for a Shut-in:

1. Spend time in conversation together. Ask about Christmases gone by. Let your friend do the talking.
2. Take a miniature decorated Christmas tree to brighten the home.
3. Offer to help your friend with shopping, wrapping, and delivering gifts.
4. Offer to make your friend's favorite Christmas cookies.
5. Invite your friend to your home for a Christmas brunch or dinner. If homebound, take your friend a warm Christmas dinner on a bright holiday plate with a small poinsettia to brighten the day.

The greatest and most momentous fact which the history of the world records is the fact of [Christ's] birth.

—Charles H. Spurgeon

Christmas Joys: A Treasury of Old Favorites and New Gems of Christmas Lo:
Legend, and Inspiration by Joan Winmill Brown
New York: Doubleday & Company, 1982.

*A*nd in the Christ-Child we behold the
Lord of Life and Love.

—Unknown

*W*ere earth a thousand times as fair,

Beset with gold and jewels rare,

She yet were far too poor to be

A narrow cradle, Lord, for Thee.

—Martin Luther

Were Earth A Thousand Times As Fair
Martin Luther
Christmas Joys: A Treasury of Old Favorites and New Gems of Christmas Lo:
Legend, and Inspiration by Joan Winmill Brown
New York: Doubleday & Company, 1982.

It is good to be children sometimes,
and never better than at Christmas,
when its mighty Founder was a child Himself.

—Charles Dickens

Children at Christmas
Charles Dickens
Christmas Joys: A Treasury of Old Favorites
and New Gems of Christmas Lo:
Legend, and Inspiration
by Joan Winmill Brown
New York: Doubleday & Company, 1982.

Fun Things Never To Give Someone Else's Kids:

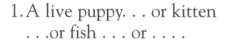

1. A live puppy. . . or kitten . . .or fish . . . or . . . .

2. A game with more than five pieces or pieces smaller than a nickel.

3. A chemistry set.

4. An incense burner with incense.

5. Tickets to a rock concert.

6. A horn . . . or symbols . . . or drums . . . or . . . .

There must be some deep psychological reason why we turn so instinctively toward home at this special time. . . . A place where every day will be Christmas, with everybody there together. At home.

—Marjorie Holmes

"Christmas at Home"
Marjorie Holmes
Christmas Joys: A Treasury of Old Favorites and New Gems of Christmas Lo:
Legend, and Inspiration by Joan Winmill Brown
New York: Doubleday & Company, 1982.

Christmas Tree Decorating Theme— Victorian:

1. White, green, and blue lights.
2. Victorian doll house furniture painted and hung on the tree.
3. Victorian dolls with fancy dresses set on the branches.
4. White, green or blue bows.
5. White flocking or heavy white snow over the branches.
6. Large white ribbon draped about the tree for garland.
7. Large Victorian doll on top.

The Greatest Christmas Ever

ROAST TURKEY WITH STUFFING

10 to 12-lb. turkey
Unsalted shortening
Salt and pepper
Paprika

*W*ash the turkey inside and out, and pat dry with a cloth. Rub the inside with salt, and fill the body cavity with the stuffing. Secure with skewers. Place the bird, breast side up, in a roasting pan. Brush the breast, legs, and wings with the shortening. Preheat oven to 300° F., and roast the turkey, uncovered, in the oven until tender, allowing 25 minutes to the pound. Baste frequently with pan drippings. When turkey is half cooked, season to taste with salt, pepper, and paprika.

—President and Mrs. Woodrow Wilson

Christmas Joys: A Treasury of Old Favorites and New Gems of Christmas Lo: Legend, and Inspiration by Joan Winmill Brown Doubleday & Company, 1982.

TENNESSEE HAM

1 ham
1 cup dark molasses
Cloves
1 1/2 cups brown sugar
Cracker crumbs
Fruit preserves

*C*ompletely cover the ham in cold water and soak overnight. Take out and remove any hard surface. Put in suitably sized pot with fresh water, skin side down; add molasses. Cook slowly (225° F.), allowing 25 minutes to the pound. Allow to cool in the liquid. Remove skin carefully. Score ham; stick a clove in each square. Sprinkle with paste made of brown sugar, meal or cracker crumbs, and sufficient liquid to make the paste. Bake slowly in moderate oven (320° F.) for 1 hour, until evenly browned. Decorate platter with thin slices cut from the roasted ham, rolled into cornucopias and filled with fruit preserves.

—President and Mrs. James K. Polk

Christmas Joys: A Treasury of Old Favorites and New Gems of Christmas Lo: Legend, and Inspiration by Joan Winmill Brown Doubleday & Company, 1982.

MASHED POTATOES

3 large Idaho potatoes
Salt to taste
1/4 tsp. pepper
2 oz. butter
2 eggs
Pastry bag

*P*eel the potatoes and cut in half. Put in a pan and cover with cold water. Add 1 tbsp. salt, bring to a boil. Let the potatoes simmer until they are soft; drain, return to pan to dry a little. Mash them until smooth, adding butter and 1 egg. Season to taste with salt and pepper. Fill pastry bag with the potato mixture. Use rose tube. Pipe large rosettes on buttered baking dish, sprinkle with beaten egg. Lightly brown under the broiler, watching carefully so that potatoes do not get too brown.

—President James Buchanan

Christmas Joys: A Treasury of Old Favorites and New Gems of Christmas Lo: Legend, and Inspiration by Joan Winmill Brown Doubleday & Company, 1982.

Boring Gifts to Never Give Your Boss for Christmas:

1. A desk calendar.

2. A daytimer.

3. A tie.

4. White handkerchiefs.

5. A Christmas T-shirt.

The Greatest Christmas Ever

JAM SESSION

*O*ne Sunday evening, I overheard my five-year-old, Julie, practicing "Hark the Herald Angels Sing," a song she'd been rehearsing that morning in church for next week's Christmas program.

It was all I could do to suppress my laughter when, in place of "which angelic hosts proclaim," Julie sang, "with the jelly toast proclaim."

—Marilyn Clark
Cincinnati, OH

"Heart to Heart:
Everyday Glimpses of Humor and Hope" —
Today's Christian (Nov./Dec. 1994)

Christmas Tree Theme— Oriental:

1. Red lights.

2. Small colorful umbrellas and fans.

3. Various types of birds, large and small, on the branches.

4. Fortune cookies tied with red ribbon for ornaments.

5. Multicolored sashes draping the tree for garland.

6. Red berries.

7. A large bright bird on top.

The Greatest Christmas Ever

THIS TOO I SHALL GIVE

*T*his is Christmas—the real meaning of it.
God loving, searching; giving Himself—to us.
Man needing; receiving, giving himself—to God.
Redemption's glorious exchange of gifts!
Without which we cannot live;
Without which we cannot give to those we love
anything of lasting value.
This is the meaning of Christmas—the wonder and
the glory of it.

—Ruth Bell Graham

Christmas Joys: A Treasury of Old Favorites and New Gems of Christmas Lo:
Legend, and Inspiration by Joan Winmill Brown
Doubleday & Company, 1982.

. . . Interpersonal relationships are the most valued and cherished gifts of all. The Bible teaches that God gave a Person as a gift to every one of us, and that Person is Jesus Christ.

—Rev. Billy Graham

Rev. Billy Graham
Christmas Joys: A Treasury of Old Favorites and New Gems of Christmas Lo:
Legend, and Inspiration by Joan Winmill Brown
Doubleday & Company, 1982.

Things Never To Give Your Wife for Christmas:

1. A frying pan, blender, or vacuum.
2. A scale—either for weighing food or her body.
3. Perfume you say you liked when you smelled it on another woman.
4. A copy of the favorite recipe your mother always made you.
5. House shoes like your mother wears.
6. A nightgown one size too small, cut to fit Twiggy, made of polyester, with sleeves that are so tight at the wrists they could pass for tourniquets.

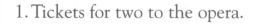

Things Never To Give Your Husband for Christmas:

1. Tickets for two to the opera.

2. Stationery.

3. Cologne you say you liked when you smelled it on another man.

4. Your favorite CD by Barbra Streisand.

5. A book on managing personal finances.

6. A red flannel night shirt.

Things Your Wife Would Love To Receive for Christmas:

1. Her favorite perfume, bath oil, and bath powder.

2. A gift certificate to her favorite shoe or clothing store.

3. A trip for two to a mountainside bed and breakfast inn.

4. A candlelit dinner for two "on the town."

5. A housekeeper twice a month for the next year.

Things Your Husband Would Love To Receive for Christmas:

1. An electric weed trimmer.

2. A gas grill.

3. His favorite cologne.

4. A candlelit home-made steak dinner for two.

5. Fur-lined leather gloves.

I saw a stable, low and very bare,
A little child in a manger.
The oxen knew Him, had Him in their care,
To men He was a stranger.
The safety of the world was lying there,
And the world's danger.

—Mary Elizabeth Coleridge

"I Saw a Stable"
Mary Elizabeth Coleridge
The Oxford Book of Christmas Poems edited by Harrison, Michael & Christop:
Clark
London: Oxford University Press, 1983.

Christmas Tree Decorating Theme— Winter:

1. Flocked tree.
2. White lights.
3. Red ornaments.
4. Red bows.
5. Red berries.
6. Red beads in strings for garland.
7. Red poinsettias.
8. Pine cones.
9. Red birds.

What can I give Him,
Poor as I am?
If I were a shepherd,
I would bring a lamb,
If I were a Wise Man
I would do my part,—
Yet what I can I give Him,
Give my heart.

—Christina G. Rossetti

A Child's Christmas Treasury by Mark Daniel
New York: Dial Books for Young Readers, 1988., 59.

DO YOU HEAR WHAT I HEAR?

*A*fter the Sunday School class had sung "Silent Night" and been told the Christmas story, the teacher suggested that her pupils draw the Nativity scene. A little boy finished first. The teacher praised his drawing of the manger, of Joseph, of Mary and the Infant. But she was puzzled by a roly-poly figure off to one side and asked who it was.

"Oh," explained the youngster, "that's Round John Virgin."

—*Reader's Digest*
(December, 1958)

The Great American Christmas Almanac:
A Complete Compendium of Facts

PEANUT BUTTER GRANOLA COOKIES

1/2 cup butter
1 egg
1/2 cup peanut butter
1/2 cup sugar
3/4 cup whole wheat flour
3/4 cup granola
1/2 teaspoon baking powder
3/4 teaspoon baking soda
1/4 teaspoon salt

*P*reheat the oven to 375° F. Grease a cookie sheet. In a mixing bowl, blend together the butter and egg. Add the remaining ingredients. Onto the cookie sheet, drop the dough by rounded teaspoonfuls. Bake 10 to 12 minutes.

—Stormie Omartian

7 LAYER COOKIES

1/2 cup melted butter
1 cup graham cracker crumbs
1 cup chocolate chip morsels
   (all milk chocolate)
1 cup butterscotch chip morsels
1 cup coconut flakes
1 cup walnuts, chopped
1 can Borden Eagle Brand
   Condensed Milk*
   [*Brand Name]

*P*reheat the oven to 325° F. Cover the bottom of a 9" x 13" pan with the melted butter. Over the butter, sprinkle the graham cracker crumbs, then layer the chocolate chips, butterscotch chips, coconut and walnuts. Pour Eagle Brand over all, then bake for 25 minutes. Let cool. Cut into squares. Refrigerate until firm, then serve.

—Beverly LaHaye

More Than A Cookbook Cookbook
by Janic Subers
Tulsa: Honor Book, 1986., 188.

46

Selfishness makes Christmas a burden; love makes it a delight.

—Unknown

Things Never To Give Your Teen for Christmas:

1. Clothes that you picked out.

2. Socks and underwear.

3. A gift certificate for books.

4. A trip with the family to an isolated cabin for the weekend.

5. Family pictures.

Things Your Teen Would Love To Receive for Christmas:

1. A gift certificate for clothes to his/her favorite store.

2. A genuine leather wallet.

3. A gift certificate for CD's.

4. A set of roller blades.

5. A mountain bike.

Eight Neat Privileges To Give Your Teen for Christmas:

1. Driving the favorite family car on one date.

2. Taking a date out for steaks one special evening "on the house."

3. Taking a late curfew one evening, time to be agreed upon with the parents.

4. Receiving a double allowance for one week.

5. Receiving two free tickets to a movie upon request.

CHOCOLATE CHIP CAKE

1 package yellow cake mix
1 package instant chocolate
   pudding mix
1/2 cup oil
1/2 cup water
4 eggs
1/2 pint sour cream
1 6-oz. pkg. chocolate chips
Small amount flour

*P*reheat the oven to 350° F. Butter a bundt pan. Combine first six ingredients. Flour the chips, then fold them into the cake mixture. Pour the batter into the bundt pan and bake for 30 minutes or until a toothpick inserted into the center comes out clean.

—Cheryl Prewitt Salem

More Than A Cookbook Cookbook
by Janic Subers
Tulsa: Honor Book, 1986., 209.

*T*he only blind person at Christmas-time
is he who has not Christmas in his heart.

—Helen Keller

The Great American Christmas Almanac:
A Complete Compendium of Facts and Traditions by Irena Chalmers
New York: The Penguin Group, 1988., 23.

*C*hristmas is telling time—wondering
time. Wonder enough about it, and you'll
know, and you'll tell about it. . . .

—Roy Rogers

The Wonder of Christmas
Roy Rogers
Christmas Joys: A Treasury of Old Favorites and New Gems of Christmas Lo:
Legend, and Inspiration by Joan Winmill Brown
New York: Doubleday & Company, 1982.

SAGE AND ONION STUFFING

1 lb. potatoes, peeled and
    halved, if large
2 tbsps. melted butter
2 medium-sized onions, peeled
    and finely chopped
2 tart apples, peeled, cored,
    and finely chopped
1 tbsp. crumbled dried sage
1 tsp. chopped fresh parsley
Salt and pepper

*P*ut the potatoes in a medium-sized saucepan, cover them with cold water, add salt, and bring to a boil. Lower the heat and simmer for 15 to 20 minutes or until just tender; drain. Dice the potatoes. Heat the butter and cook the onions and apples for 8 minutes until they have softened. Stir in the diced potatoes and the herbs. Season to taste with salt and pepper. Fill the stuffing into the cavity of the turkey or goose.

Creative Ways To Personalize Your Christmas Cards:

1. Tape a family picture inside.
2. Enclose a favorite family recipe on a 3 x 5 card, with the name of the relative you associate with it.
3. Enclose a one-page Holiday Update to share what's going on in your family.
4. Copy and enclose a cherished family holiday poem.
5. Inside the cover, pen your favorite Scripture focusing on Jesus.

HOME-MADE EGGNOG

12 large eggs
1 can evaporated skim milk,
   13 oz.
1 cup confectioner's sugar
Nutmeg

*B*eat the eggs together in a large bowl until foamy. Add milk and sugar. Stir. Strain mixture through sieve and pour into jar. Close lid and chill. Sprinkle nutmeg on top when ready to serve.

If . . . we open our hearts and embrace Him . . . not only to reap abundance and joy and health and happy fulfillment, but also for the cancellation of our sins—then this is the greatest welcome we can give to the Christ Child.

—Norman Vincent Peale

The Greatest Welcome
Norman Vincent Peale
The Guideposts Christmas Treasury
New York: Doubleday & Company, 1980.

THE NATIVITY

*A*mong the oxen (like an ox I'm slow)
I see a glory in the stable grow
Which, with the ox's dullness might at length
    Give me an ox's strength.

Among the asses (stubborn I as they)
I see my Savior where I looked for hay;
So may my beastlike folly learn at least
    The patience of a beast.

Among the sheep (I like a sheep have strayed)
I watch the manger where my Lord is laid;
Oh that my baa-ing nature would win thence
    Some woolly innocence!

—C. S. Lewis

Permission given by Harcourt Brace Jovanovich

When we receive Christ, we experience completely the gift that is Christmas. Then, for us, Christmas is truly always, for Jesus said, Lo, I am with you always... And Christmas is Jesus!

—Dale Evans Rogers

The Guideposts Christmas Treasury.
New York: Doubleday & Company, 1980.

A CHRISTMAS PRAYER

*L*oving Father, help us remember the birth of Jesus, that we may share in the song of angels, the gladness of the shepherds, and the worship of the wise men. Close the door of hate and open the door of love all over the world. Let kindness come with every gift and good desires with every greeting. Deliver us from evil by the blessing which Christ brings, and teach us to be merry with clear hearts. May the Christmas morning make us happy to be Thy children, and the Christmas evening bring us to our beds with grateful thoughts, forgiving and forgiven, for Jesus' sake. Amen!

—Robert Louis Stevenson

Christmas Joys: A Treasury of Old Favorites and New Gems of Christmas Lo:
Legend, and Inspiration by Joan Winmill Brown
New York: Doubleday & Company, 1982

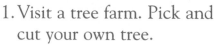

Christmas Tree Theme— Country:

1. Visit a tree farm. Pick and cut your own tree.
2. String popcorn and berries for garland.
3. Hang glittered pine cones and small wooden children's toys for ornaments.
4. Cut out construction paper candy canes, stars and bells; glue on glitter, and hang.
5. Make a pine-cone angel for the top.
6. Put plenty of candles in safe candleholders on your hearth and on tables close by for lighting.

. . . None will ever find a way
To banish Christ from Christmas Day. . .
For with each child there's born again
A Mystery that baffles men.

—Helen Steiner Rice

The Miracle of Christmas
Helen Steiner Rice
The Guideposts Christmas Treasury.
New York: Doubleday & Company, 1980.

CINNAMON CHRISTMAS TREES

2 pkgs. refrigerated cinnamon
   rolls with icing, 9 1/2 oz. ea.
6 tbsps. granola, raisins, or nuts

Preheat oven to 375° F. Cover a 10" x 14" baking sheet with foil. Separate rolls. Arrange rolls in rows to simulate a Christmas tree. Starting at the center top of baking sheet, set rolls very closely in rows of 1-2-3-4-5. Bake 18 to 20 minutes. Remove from oven. While rolls are hot, spread with icing and sprinkle with granola, raisins, or nuts to decorate.

Used by permission of Ideals Children's Books, an imprint of Hambleton-Hill Publishing, Inc.

THE LEGEND OF THE CHRISTMAS ROSE

*L*egend says that a little shepherd girl of Bethlehem followed after the shepherds who had received the angels' message and were journeying to the stable. All the shepherds took along gifts for the Christ child, but the little girl had no gift to give. As she lagged behind the others, somewhat sad at heart, there suddenly appeared an angel in a glow of light, who scattered beautiful white roses in her path. Eagerly she gathered them in her arms and laid them at the manger as her gift to the little Lord Jesus.

—Unknown

Author Unknown
A Child's Christmas Treasury by Mark Daniel
New York: Dial Books for Young Readers, 1988., 29.

CINNAMON BELLS

1 tbsp. ground cinnamon
2 tbsps. sugar
Several slices of hot buttered
   toast
Cookie Cutter—Christmas bell

*C*ut the bread with the Christmas bell cookie cutter. Toast with butter. Mix the spice and sugar together. Sprinkle the mixture on the hot buttered toast.

Author Unknown
A Child's Christmas Treasury by Mark Daniel
New York: Dial Books for Young Readers,
1988., 57.

Gifts for Those Special Persons Who Have Everything:

1. A gift certificate that relates to an area of special interest.

2. A book that relates to an area of special interest.

3. A magazine subscription that relates to an area of special interest.

4. A gift packet of movie tickets to a local theater.

5. A gift certificate for a dinner for two to an elegant, local restaurant.

TIME OF ENCHANTMENT

On Christmas Eve, the story says, an enchantment falls upon the earth. It is a time when the Spirit of a new-born Child whose name is Love, possesses the world. The way to Christmas lies through an ancient gate . . . . It is a little gate, child-high, child-wide, and there is a password: "Peace on earth to men of good will." May you, this Christmas, become as a little child again and enter into His kingdom.

—Angelo Patri

CHRISTMAS CUSTARD WITH BANANA SAUCE

2 cups skim milk
2 eggs
1/4 cup sugar
1/2 tsp. rum extract
1/4 cup currant jelly
1 medium ripe banana

*I*n 2-qt. saucepan with wire whisk, combine skim milk, eggs, and sugar. Cook over low heat until mixture thickens and coats spoon well (do not boil or mixture will curdle) about 20 minutes, stirring constantly. Stir in rum extract. Spoon custard into four 8-oz. goblets or dessert dishes. Cover and refrigerate mixture until well chilled, about 1 hour. *To serve:* In 1-qt. saucepan over low heat, melt currant jelly. Remove saucepan from heat. Dice banana; gently stir banana into melted jelly. Spoon 1/4 of banana mixture onto each serving of chilled custard.

The Greatest Christmas Ever

LONG WALK PART OF GIFT

*T*he African boy listened carefully as the teacher explained why it is that Christians give presents to each other on Christmas day. "The gift is an expression of our joy over the birth of Jesus and our friendship for each other," she said.

When Christmas day came, the boy brought to the teacher a sea shell of lustrous beauty. "Where did you ever find such a beautiful shell?" the teacher asked as she gently fingered the gift.

The youth told her that there was only one spot where such extraordinary shells could be found. When he named the place, a certain bay several miles away, the teacher was left speechless.

"Why...why, it's gorgeous...wonderful, but you shouldn't have gone all that way to get a gift for me."

His eyes brightening, the boy answered, "Long walk part of gift."

—Gerald Horton Bath

MAPLE BREAD PUDDING

1 tbsp. butter or margarine
3 cups fresh bread cubes
  (about 6 to 8 slices)
1 1/4 cups maple syrup or
  maple-blended syrup
4 eggs
1 cup half-and-half
1/2 cup milk
2 tbsps. sugar
1 1/2 tsps. vanilla extract
1 1/4 tsps. salt

*G*rease 1 1/2-qt. casserole. In 2 quart saucepan over medium-low heat, melt butter. Stir in bread cubes; gently toss to coat well. Pour into casserole; pour 1/2 cup maple syrup over bread cubes in casserole. In medium bowl with fork, beat eggs with next 5 ingredients; pour this mixture over the bread-cube mixture. Set casserole in 9" x 9" baking pan; place pan on oven rack. Pour hot water in pan to come halfway up side of casserole. Bake in 350° F. oven 1 hour and 15 minutes or until knife inserted in center comes out clean. *To serve*, in small saucepan heat remaining maple syrup until hot. Invert pudding onto warm plate. Serve pudding warm with hot syrup.

The Good Housekeeping All-American Cookbook
New York: Hearst Books, 1987., 298.

The Greatest Christmas Ever

THE RESPONSIBILITY

*L*et the children have their night of fun and laughter, let the gifts of Father Christmas delight their play. Let us grown-ups share to the full in their unstinted pleasures before we turn again to the stern tasks and the formidable years that lie before us, resolved that by our sacrifice and daring these same children shall not be robbed of their inheritance or denied their right to live in a free and decent world. And so, in God's mercy, a happy Christmas to you all.

—Winston Churchill

Let Us Celebrate Christmas
Winston Churchill
Christmas Joys: A Treasury of Old Favorites and New Gems of Christmas Lo:
Legend, and Inspiration by Joan Winmill Brown
New York: Doubleday & Company, 1982.

THAT AGELESS MAGIC

*O*ne recent Christmas I was visiting my parents who live in a mining community in West Virginia. Times were bad. I noticed in front of me, a young couple stopped near a lame man. The husband, obviously a miner, and his wife were talking in half whispers. The young husband looked down at his wife. Slowly, a smile came over his face and he agreed. She pulled out an old black change purse. Then she walked slowly to the lame man and turned the purse upside down. Coins rattled noisily into the old man's cup. "I'm wishin' you a Merry Christmas," she whispered. Gratefully, the lame man reached out to shake her hand.

I watched them walk down the street. They were broke and would have to walk home. But I could tell by the bounce in their steps that it would not be a long walk. When they lightened their purse, they also lightened their hearts, and the joy that comes from giving had worked its ageless magic once again.

—Loren Young

READY FOR CHRISTMAS

"Ready for Christmas," she said with a sigh
As she gave a last touch to the gifts piled high. . .
Then wearily sat for a moment to read
Till soon, very soon, she was nodding her head.
Then quietly spoke a voice in her dream,
"Ready for Christmas, what do you mean? . . ."
She woke with a start and a cry of despair.
"There's so little time and I've still to prepare.
Oh, Father! Forgive me, I see what You mean!
To be ready means more than a house swept clean.
Yes, more than the giving of gifts and a tree.
It's the heart swept clean that He wanted to see,
A heart that is free from bitterness and sin.
So be ready for Christmas—and ready for Him."

—Unknown

The Greatest Christmas Ever

HOLIDAY PECAN CRUNCH

2 cups all-purpose flour
1 cup packed light brown sugar
1 cup butter or margarine,
    softened
1 egg
1 tsp. vanilla extract
1 pkg. semi-sweet
    chocolate pieces, 6 oz.
1 1/2 cups pecans, toasted
    and chopped

*I*nto large bowl, measure first 5 ingredients. With hand, knead dough until well blended and it holds together. Preheat oven to 350° F. Pat dough evenly into 15 1/2" x 10 1/2" jelly-roll pan. Bake 25 minutes. In small saucepan over low heat, melt chocolate, stirring frequently; set aside. Remove pan from oven; pour chocolate over baked layer; with spatula, evenly spread over; sprinkle with pecans. Cool on wire rack. When cool, cut lengthwise into 6 strips, cut each strip crosswise into 12 pieces. Store in tightly-covered container; use up within 1 week.

Used by permission of William-Morrow
An Imprint of William-Morrow

The Greatest Christmas Ever

LEGEND OF THE CHRISTMAS TREE

*T*here is a legend that comes down to us from the early days of Christianity in England. One of those helping to spread Christianity among the Druids was a monk named Wilfred (later Saint Wilfred).

One day, surrounded by a group of his converts, he struck down a huge oak tree, which, in the Druid religion, was an object of worship. As it fell to the earth, the oak tree split into four pieces and from its center sprung up a young fir tree.

Wilfred turned to speak, "This little tree shall be your Holy Tree tonight. It is the wood of peace, for your houses are built of the fir. It is the sign of an endless life, for its leaves are evergreen. See how it points toward the heavens? Let this be called the tree of the Christ Child. Gather about it, not in the wilderness, but in your homes. There it will be surrounded with loving gifts and rites of kindness."

To this day, that is why the fir tree is one of our loveliest symbols of Christmas.

—Unknown

CELEBRATION MELTAWAYS

2 jars macadamia nuts,
   7 1/2 oz. ea.
2 cups flour, all-purpose
1 cup butter or margarine,
   softened
1/4 cup confectioners' sugar
1 tsp. almond extract

*I*n blender at medium speed, blend 1 cup nuts until finely ground; place in large bowl. Reserve remaining nuts for tops. Into bowl with ground nuts, measure remaining ingredients. Knead until blended and dough holds together. Preheat oven to 350° F. With hands, shape scant tablespoonfuls of dough into balls. Place 1 inch apart on ungreased cookie sheets; press reserved nuts into tops. Bake 12 to 15 minutes, until lightly browned. Remove to wire racks; cool.

Used by permission of William-Morrow
An Imprint of William-Morrow

One summer my family gave work to a wandering man. In the fall he left us, but at Christmas a greeting card arrived from hundreds of miles away—no personal message, just a signature. Then in the spring, he came to see us.

"I've stopped drinking," he said. "I'm going to a permanent job." When we thanked him for his Christmas card, he told us that it was the only card he had sent. "I wanted it to say 'Thank you,' not for the work, but for the respect you gave me. It helped me to begin a new life."

—Reamer Kline

CHRISTMAS SPRITZ

3 cups all-purpose flour
1 1/2 cups butter or margarine,
   softened
1 egg
3/4 cup sugar
1/4 cup orange juice
Powdered sugar

*I*nto large bowl, measure all ingredients. With mixer at low speed, beat until blended, scraping bowl with rubber spatula. Preheat oven to 375° F. Using cookie press, fitted with bar-plate tip, press dough into strips, 1 inch apart, for length of ungreased cookie sheet. Bake 8 minutes, until light golden. Immediately cut each strip crosswise into 2 1/2-inch cookies. With metal spatula, remove to wire racks to cool. Sprinkle with powdered sugar. Repeat with remaining dough.

Used by permission of William-Morrow
An Imprint of William-Morrow

There was a lady in the state hospital. She carried the card a friend of ours sent her in a little draw-string bag and during the entire Christmas season she would stop people and say, "Look at my Christmas card. The lady I worked for sent it to me. I'm not forgotten." We heard later that card, the only one she received, was the beginning of her recovery.

—Reamer Kline

DUTCH CHRISTMAS BUTTER COOKIES

2 1/2 cups all-purpose flour
1 cup sugar
1 cup butter, softened
1 1/2 tsp baking powder
1 tsp vanilla extract
1/2 tsp salt
1 egg
1 egg yolk
2 tbsps water
1/4 cup candied ginger, chopped

*I*nto large bowl, measure first 7 ingredients. With mixer at low speed, beat until blended. With hands, on waxed paper, roll into three 6"-long rolls. Flatten each slightly to shape into a bar. Wrap; refrigerate 2 hours or up to 1 week. Preheat oven to 350° F. Grease cookie sheets. In cup with fork, beat yolk with water. Slice one roll of dough at a time crosswise into 1/4"-thick slices. Place, 1 inch apart, on cookie sheets. Brush each cookie with egg-yolk mixture and press chopped ginger into tops. Bake 10 minutes, until lightly browned. With spatula, remove to wire racks to cool.

Fun Gift Exchanges:

1. *White elephants.* Something used, but useful.
2. *Favorite book.* Write in the front what it has meant to you.
3. *Cookies.* Bring 1/2 dozen of your favorite Christmas cookie and the recipe on a 3 x 5 card for *each* person attending.
4. *Ornaments.* Unique and under $5.00 each.
5. *Picture frames.* Unique and under $5.00 each.

SCRUMPTIOUS PUMPKIN BREAD

3 cups flour, all-purpose
1 1/2 cups sugar
1 1/2 tsps. cinnamon, ground
1 tsp. baking soda
1 tsp. salt
3/4 tsp. nutmeg,
 ground
3/4 tsp. cloves, ground
1/2 tsp. baking powder
3 eggs
1 can pumpkin, 16 oz.
1 cup salad oil
1 cup golden or dark raisins,
 seedless
1/2 cup walnuts, chopped

*P*reheat oven to 350° F. Grease two 8 1/2" x 4 1/2" loaf pans. In large bowl with fork, mix first 8 ingredients. In medium bowl with fork, beat eggs, pumpkin, and salad oil until blended; stir into flour mixture just until flour is moistened. Stir in raisins and walnuts. Spoon evenly into loaf pans. Bake 1 hour 15 minutes or until toothpick inserted comes out clean. Cool in pans on rack 10 minutes; remove from pans; cool on rack.

Sentimental Gifts for Loved Ones:

1. Ornaments home-made out of old lace tablecloths.

2. A favorite family recipe passed down through the generations.

3. A piece of art made of the children's handprints and fingerpaint.

4. Cuttings from your favorite greenhouse plants, potted in a small vase that is wrapped in a holiday bow.

5. This book.

Christmas is a time to remember the gift of God's giving nature in every area of life. He gave us earth to live on, fellow humans to love, work and share with, and great meaning in life — to serve our fellow man. The gift of God's Son Jesus gives us peace to enjoy all these other gifts as His family on earth — and to live in eternal joy. Merry Christmas to us who have received all God's gifts. Joy to the World!

—Unknown

Handmade Gift for Kids To Make and Give— Country Christmas Candle:

1. Select a round narrow log. Saw the log into 2-inch deep rounds.
2. Collect small pine cones and other dried nature items.
3. Cut a small hole the size of a candle in the center of each round.
4. Hot glue the dried nature items around the center hole.
5. Stabilize a red slender candle in the center hole.
6. Wrap a plaid ribbon around the bottom of the candle and glue felt to the bottom.

Christmas Tree Decorating Theme— North Pole:

1. Flocked tree.

2. White lights.

3. Ornaments: little toys, candy canes, trains, horns, soldiers, elves, reindeer, and sleighs.

4. Miniature cottages with chimneys.

5. Mr. and Mrs. Santas of all shapes and sizes.

6. Miniature gifts and packages.

7. Red and green ribbon for garland.

Treats Never To Leave Santa on Christmas Eve:

1. Hot soup. (It gets cold.)

2. Milk. (It gets hot.)

3. Cookies. (He gets those everywhere.)

4. Candies. (He needs to lose that tummy.)

5. Sandwich. (The bread dries out.)

Treats Santa Would Love To Find on Christmas Eve:

1. Aged cheeses with a variety of crackers.

2. Smoked oysters and salmon on toast points.

3. Boiled shrimp on ice with cocktail sauce.

4. Mushrooms stuffed with crabmeat.

5. Chips and fresh salsa with guacamole.

And I do come home at Christmas. We all do, or we all should. We all come home, or ought to come home, for a short holiday—the longer, the better—from the great boarding school, where we are forever working at our arithmetical slates, to take, and give a rest.

—Charles Dickens

Charles Dickens
Your Attitude Determines Your Attitude.
Success Collection Quote Books., 21.

Gifts Your Dog and Cat Hate To Receive at Christmas:

1. A bath.

2. Perfume.

3. A bow.

4. A bulky coat.

5. A formal portrait with the family.

Gifts Your Dog Loves To Receive at Christmas:

1. A fuzzy ball.
2. A flavored, rawhide chew stick.
3. A lightweight winter sweater.
4. A chance to snack on leftovers.
5. A comfy pillow to sleep on.

Gifts Your Cat Loves To Receive at Christmas:

1. Tidbits of turkey, chicken, and ham.

2. Solitude.

3. A scratching post.

4. Lots of balls!

" *D*o unto others as you would have them do unto you!" *(Matthew 7:12.)*

The Greatest Christmas Ever

O little town of Bethlehem,
How still we see thee lie!
Above thy deep and dreamless sleep
The silent stars go by;
Yet in thy dark streets shineth
The everlasting Light;
The hopes and fears of all the years
Are met in thee tonight.

—Phillip Brooks

The Sword Scrapbook II by Viola Walden
Tennessee: Sword of the Lord Publishers, 1975., 31.

$\mathcal{D}$eck the hall with boughs of holly,
    Fa-la-la-la-la, la-la-la-la;
'Tis the season to be jolly,
    Fa-la-la-la-la, la-la-la-la;
Don we now our gay apparel,
    Fa-la-la, fa-la-la, la-la-la.
Troll the ancient Yuletide carol.
    Fa-la-la-la-la, la-la-la-la.
—Traditional Welsh Carol

The Holly and the Ivy: A Celebration of Christmas
by Barbara Segall
New York: Clarkson Potter/Publishers, 1991., 23.

The Greatest Christmas Ever

Joy to the world! the Lord is come:
Let earth receive her King;
Let ev'ry heart prepare Him room,
And heav'n and nature sing.

He rules the world with truth and grace,
And makes the nations prove
The glories of His righteousness,
And wonders of His love.

—Isaac Watts

Christmas Joys: A Treasury of Old Favorites and New Gems of Christmas Lo:
Legend, and Inspiration by Joan Winmill Brown
New York: Doubleday & Company, 1982.

Away in a manger, no crib for a bed,
The little Lord Jesus laid down His sweet head;
The stars in the sky looked down where He lay,
The little Lord Jesus asleep on the hay.

The cattle are lowing, the Baby awakes,
But little Lord Jesus, no crying He makes;
I love Thee, Lord Jesus! look down from the sky,
And stay by my cradle till morning is nigh.

—Attributed to Martin Luther

JINGLE BELLS

*D*ashing through the snow
In a one-horse open sleigh,
O'er the fields we go
Laughing all the way.
Bells on bobtail ring,
Making spirits bright.
What fun it is to ride and sing
A sleighing song tonight!
CHORUS:
Jingle bells! Jingle bells!
Jingle all the way!
Oh, what fun it is to ride in a one-horse open sleigh!
Jingle bells! Jingle bells!
Jingle all the way!
Oh, what fun it is to ride in a one-horse open sleigh!

—James Pierpont

The Greatest Christmas Ever

O COME, ALL YE FAITHFUL

O come, all ye faithful, joyful and triumphant;
O come ye, O come ye to Bethlehem;
Come and behold Him, born the King of angels!

Sing, choirs of angels, sing in exultation,
O sing, all ye bright hosts of heav'n above!
Glory to God, all glory in the highest!

Yea, Lord, we greet Thee, born this happy morning,
Jesus, to Thee be all glory giv'n;
Word of the Father, now in flesh appearing!

Refrain: O come, let us adore Him, Christ the Lord.

—Latin hymn
English translation by
Frederick Oakley

Amazing Grace: 366 Inspiring Hymn Stories for Daily Devotions by Kenneth Osbeck
Michigan: Kregel Publications, 1990., 367.

The Greatest Christmas Ever

WHAT CHILD IS THIS?

*W*hat Child is this, Who, laid to rest, on Mary's lap is sleeping?

Whom angels greet with anthems sweet, While shepherds watch are keeping?

This, this is Christ, the King, Whom shepherds guard and angels sing;

Haste, haste to bring Him laud, the Babe, the Son of Mary.

Why lies He in such mean estate where ox and ass are feeding?

Good Christian, fear, for sinners here the silent Word is pleading.

So bring Him incense, gold and myrrh, come, peasant king to own Him;

The King of kings salvation brings, let loving hearts enthrone Him.

—William C. Dix

Amazing Grace: 366 Inspiring Hymn Stories for Daily Devotions by Kenneth Osbeck
Michigan: Kregel Publications, 1990., 369.

Now all this was done, that it might be fulfilled which was spoken of the Lord by the prophet, saying, Behold, a virgin shall be with child, and shall bring forth a son, and they shall call his name Emmanuel, which being interpreted is, God with us.

—Matthew 1:22,23

So remember while December
Brings the only Christmas Day,
In the year let there be Christmas
In the things you do and say;
Wouldn't life be worth the living
Wouldn't dreams be coming true
If we kept the Christmas spirit
All the whole year through?

—Unknown

That you may hold forever in your heart the golden memories of every happy Christmas Day you have ever known.

—Patrick F. Scanlan

Used by permission of The Tablet Publication
Brooklyn, New York

CHRISTMAS CORN

2 cans whole kernel corn,
   undrained, 16 oz. ea.
1 jar diced pimiento, drained,
   4 oz.
1 can whole mushrooms,
   drained, 4 oz.
1 1/2 tsps. dried parsley flakes

*C*ombine all ingredients in a large saucepan; cook over medium heat until thoroughly heated. Serve with a slotted spoon.

—*Southern Living*

Used by permission of Oxmoor House
An Imprint of Oxmoore House Publishing
Gary Wright, Publicity Manager

The Greatest Christmas Ever

THE BETHELEHEM STAR

*S*oft winds are blowing
O'er Bethlehem town,
Brightly the stars
From Heaven look down,
Quietly the shepherds
Their long vigil keep,
Over their flocks
Of slumbering sheep.
Hark! there's a sound
On the pulsating air,
Music is stealing
From voices somewhere.
And a beautiful light
As a star settles down
O'er a stable that stands
At the edge of the town!

—Unknown

CHRISTMAS PUDDING

2 cups flour
2 level tsps. baking powder
1/4 tsp. each ground cloves
   and cinnamon
1/2 tsp. each mace and salt
1 cup flour
1/2 pound beef suet
1/2 pound raisins
1/2 pound currants
2 ounces citron, cut fine
1 cup sugar
1 grated lemon rind
2 eggs
1/2 cup milk

*S*ift together, 3 times, flour, baking powder, spices and salt. Chop fine the suet, mixing it with the one cup of flour; add the fruit, sugar, lemon rind, and the flour mixture together. Mix thoroughly, then stir in eggs beaten very lightly and mixed with the milk. Should be quite stiff. Steam on low heat six hours in a buttered two-quart mold, in a kettle of water on a rack. Serve with hard sauce or custard.

Author Unknown
Christmas Joys: A Treasury of Old Favorites and New Gems of Christmas Lo:
Legend, and Inspiration
by Joan Winmill Brown
New York: Doubleday & Company, 1982.

When Christ was born in Bethlehem,
*   God was with us.*
When Jesus is reborn in our hearts,
*   God is with us.*
When we face the challenges of each day,
*   God is with us.*
As we look forward to a new year,
*   God is certainly with us.*

—Dayspring Collection

THE GLORY OF AND GRACE IN THE CHURCH

*C*ome now behold
With this Knot What Flowers do grow:
Spangled like gold:
Whence Wreaths of all Perfumes do flow.
Most Curious Colours of all sorts you shall
With all Sweet Spirits scent. Yet that's not all...

But as they stand
Like Beauties reaching in perfume
A Divine Hand
Doth hand them up to Glories room:
Where Each in sweet'ned Songs all Praises shall
Sing all ore Heaven for aye. And that's but all.

—Edward Taylor

The American Tradition in Literature, 4th ed. Edited by Sculley Bradley
New York: Grossett & Dunlap, 1956., 40-41.

Some say that ever 'gainst that season comes,
Wherein our Saviour's birth is celebrated.
The bird of dawning singeth all night long;
And then, they say, no spirit can walk abroad;
The nights are wholesome; then no planets
strike,
No fairy takes, nor witch hath power to
charm,
So hallow'd and so gracious is the time.

—William Shakespeare

*G*ood news: but if you ask me what it is,

I know not;

It is a track of feet in the snow,

It is a lantern showing a path,

It is a door set open.

—G. K. Chesterton

Xmas Day
G. K. Chesterton
A Christmas Album by Sam Elder
New York: Harper & Row, 1986.

Green grow'th the holly,
    So doth the ivy;
Though winter blasts blow ne'er so high,
    Green grow'th the holly.

Green grow'th the holly,
    So doth the ivy;
The God of life can never die,
    Hope! saith the holly.

—Attributed to King Henry
VIII, from a 16th-century
English carol

Christmas Magic
King Henry VIII
The Holly and the Ivy: A Celebration of Christmas by Barbara Segall
New York: Clarkson Potter/Publishers, 1991., 9.

I believe . . . in Jesus Christ His only Son our Lord; who was conceived by the Holy Ghost, born of the Virgin Mary....

I Believe…
Apostolic Creed
Christmas Joys: A Treasury of Old Favorites and New Gems of Christmas Lo:
Legend, and Inspiration by Joan Winmill Brown
New York: Doubleday & Company, 1982.

THE MESSENGERS OF GOD

*A*nd there were in the same country shepherds abiding in the field, keeping watch over their flock by night. And, lo, the angel of the Lord came upon them, and the glory of the Lord shone round about them: and they were sore afraid. And the angel said unto them, Fear not: for, behold, I bring you good tidings of great joy, which shall be to all people. For unto you is born this day in the city of David a Saviour, which is Christ the Lord. And this shall be a sign unto you; Ye shall find the babe wrapped in swaddling clothes, lying in a manger. And suddenly there was with the angel a multitude of the heavenly host praising God, and saying, Glory to God in the highest, and on earth peace, good will toward men.

—Luke 2:8-14

HOT SPICED CIDER

1 quart apple cider
1 2-inch cinnamon stick
1 nutmeg, whole
3 to 4 cloves, whole
3 to 4 allspice
1/2 tsp. orange peel, grated

*C*ombine all ingredients in a medium-sized saucepan. Bring to a boil. Turn heat to low and simmer 5 minutes. (Longer simmering makes a stronger flavor.) Serve in mugs. Decorate with a cinnamon stick in each mug.

Used by permission of Ideal's Children's Books
An Imprint of Hambleton-Hill Publishing, Inc.

THE THREE KINGS

Three Kings came riding from far away,
    Melchior and Gaspar and Baltasar;
Three Wise Men out of the East were they,
And they traveled by night and they slept by day,
    For their guide was a beautiful, wonderful star.

The star was so beautiful, large and clear,
    That all the other stars of the sky
Became a white mist in the atmosphere;
And by this they knew that the coming was near
    Of the Prince foretold in the prophecy.

—Henry Wadsworth Longfellow

Used by permission of Ideal's Children's Books
An Imprint of Hambleton-Hill Publishing, Inc.

THE GIFT OF LOVE

*I*n the beginning was the Word, and the Word was with God, and the Word was God. He was with God in the beginning. Through him all things were made; without him nothing was made that has been made. In him was life, and that life was the light of men. The light shines in the darkness, but the darkness has not understood it. He came unto his own, and his own received him not...He came to that which was his own, but his own did not receive him. Yet to all who received him, to those who believed in his name, he gave the right to become children of God—children born not of natural descent, nor of human decision or a husband's will, but born of God. The Word became flesh and made his dwelling among us. We have seen his glory, the glory of the One and Only, who came from the Father, full of grace and truth.

—John 1:1-5, 11-14 (NIV)

GOLDEN SUGAR COOKIES

2 1/2 cups flour, sifted
1 tsp. baking soda
1 tsp. cream of tartar
1/4 tsp. salt
1 cup butter, softened, unsalted
1 tsp. vanilla
1/2 tsp. lemon extract
2 cups sugar
3 egg yolks

*P*reheat oven to 350° F. Combine flour, soda, cream of tartar, and salt. Set aside. Cream butter, vanilla, and lemon extract until butter is soft and smooth. Gradually add sugar to creamed mixture, beating until fluffy. Add egg yolks, one at a time, beating well after each addition. Add dry ingredients, a little at a time, to the creamed mixture, beating after each addition until blended. Form dough into 1" balls. Place about 2" apart on ungreased cookie sheet. Bake for 10 minutes or until golden brown.

Used by permissin of Ideal's Children's Books
An Imprint of Hambleton-Hill Publishing, Inc.

GERMAN SNICKERDOODLES

2 2/3 cups flour, all-purpose
1 cup butter or margarine,
    softened
2 tsps. cream of tartar
1 tsp. baking soda
1/2 tsp. salt
1/2 tsp. vanilla extract
2 eggs
2 tsps. cinnamon, ground
Sugar

*I*nto large bowl, measure first 7 ingredients and 1 1/4 cups sugar. With mixer at low speed, beat until blended, occasionally scraping bowl with rubber spatula. Shape dough into a ball; wrap with plastic wrap. Refrigerate 2 hours, until easy to handle. Preheat oven to 400° F. In small bowl, mix cinnamon with 2 tablespoons sugar. With hands, shape dough into 1 1/2" balls. Roll dough balls in cinnamon mixture to coat lightly. Place dough balls, about 2 inches apart, on ungreased large cookie sheets. With dull edge of knife, mark each cookie several times if you like. Bake 10 to 12 minutes until lightly browned. Remove to wire racks to cool.

Used by permission of William-Morrow
An Imprint of William-Morrow

*T*his is the month, and this the happy morn,

Wherein the Son of Heaven's eternal King,

Of wedded maid and virgin mother born,

Our great redemption from above did bring;

For so the holy sages once did sing,

    That He our deadly forfeit should release;

And with His Father work us a perpetual

peace. . . .

On the Morning of Christ's Nativity
John Milton
Christmas Joys: A Treasury of Old Favorites and New Gems of Christmas Lo:
Legend, and Inspiration by Joan Winmill Brown
New York: Doubleday & Company, 1982.

HOLIDAY SUGAR COOKIES

3 1/4 cups flour, all-purpose
1 1/2 cups sugar
2/3 cup shortening
2 eggs
2 1/2 tsps. baking powder
2 tbsps. milk
1 tsp. vanilla extract
1/2 tsp. salt
Heavy or whipping cream
Non pareils or other toppings,
    to garnish
Christmas cookie cutters

*I*nto large bowl, measure first 8 ingredients. With mixer at medium speed, beat until well mixed, occasionally scraping bowl. Shape into ball; wrap; refrigerate 3 hours, until easy to handle. Preheat oven to 400° F. Grease cookie sheets. On floured surface, roll half of dough; refrigerate rest. For crisp cookies, roll paper thin; for soft cookies, roll 1/4-inch thick. With floured cookie cutters, cut dough into shapes; re-roll trimmings and cut more shapes. Place 1/2 inch apart on cookie sheets. Brush tips with cream; sprinkle with choice of colorful toppings; bake 8 minutes or until very light brown. With pancake turner remove to racks; cool.

Used by permission of
William-Morrow
An Imprint of William-Morrow

The Greatest Christmas Ever

It is Christmas in the mansion,
Yule-log fires and silken frocks:
It is Christmas in the cottage,
Mother's filling little socks.

It is Christmas on the highway,
In the thronging, busy mart;
But the dearest, truest Christmas
Is the Christmas in the heart.

—Unknown

Ah, Lord, Who hast created all,
How hast Thou made Thee weak and small,
That Thou must choose Thy infant bed
Where ass and ox but lately fed?

—Martin Luther

Lord of Creation, Weak and Small
Martin Luther
Christmas Joys: A Treasury of Old Favorites and New Gems of Christmas Lo:
Legend, and Inspiration by Joan Winmill Brown
New York: Doubleday & Company, 1982.

Neat Things To Do in the Snow— Make Snow Ice Cream:

1. Scoop clean snow off the top of a snow pile and put in large mixing bowl. [Do not eat yellow snow!]

2. Add vanilla to taste.

3. Add cream or half 'n half in small quantities to mix.

4. Add sugar to taste.

5. Mix well, and place in freezer until almost set and ready to eat.

. . .Garnished with ribbons, blithely trowls
There the huge sirloin reeked. Hard by
Plum-porridge stood, and Christmas pye;
Nor failed Old Scotland to produce
At such high-tide, her savory goose. . . .

—Sir Walter Scott

Christmas in the Olden Times
Sir Walter Scott
Christmas Joys: A Treasury of Old Favorites and New Gems of Christmas Lo:
Legend, and Inspiration by Joan Winmill Brown
New York: Doubleday & Company, 1982.

I never realized God's birth before,
How He grew likest God in being born . . .
Such ever was love's way—to rise, it stoops.

—Robert Browning

Love's Way
Robert Browning
Christmas Joys: A Treasury of Old Favorites and New Gems of Christmas Lo:
Legend, and Inspiration by Joan Winmill Brown
New York: Doubleday & Company, 1982.

FROSTED SNOWMEN

2 cups flour, all-purpose
1 cup sugar
1/2 cup shortening
1/3 cup honey
1 tsp. baking soda
2 eggs
2 cups quick-cooking oats, uncooked
1/2 cup walnuts, finely chopped
2 cups confectioners' sugar
1/4 tsp. cream of tartar
2 egg whites
Decorations: chocolate, 3/4 tsp. salt, cinnamon, and silver decors, sugar crystals

*I*nto large bowl, measure first 7 ingredients. With mixer at low speed, beat until blended. With wooden spoon, stir in oats and walnuts. Preheat oven to 375° F. With floured hands, shape mixture into thirty-six 1-inch balls and thirty-six 3/4-inch balls. Place 1" balls, 2 1/2" apart, on ungreased cookie sheets; then place 3/4" balls 1/2 inch above 1-inch balls. Bake 10 to 12 minutes, until golden. With metal spatula, remove to wire racks to cool. *Prepare frosting:* In medium bowl with mixer at low speed, beat confectioners' sugar, cream of tartar, and egg whites until blended. Increase speed to high and beat 1 minute. Dip front of each into frosting to cover. Place frosted side up, on wire racks; decorate quickly. Let frosting dry, about 1 hour.

Honor Books
P. O. Box 55388
Tulsa, OK 74155